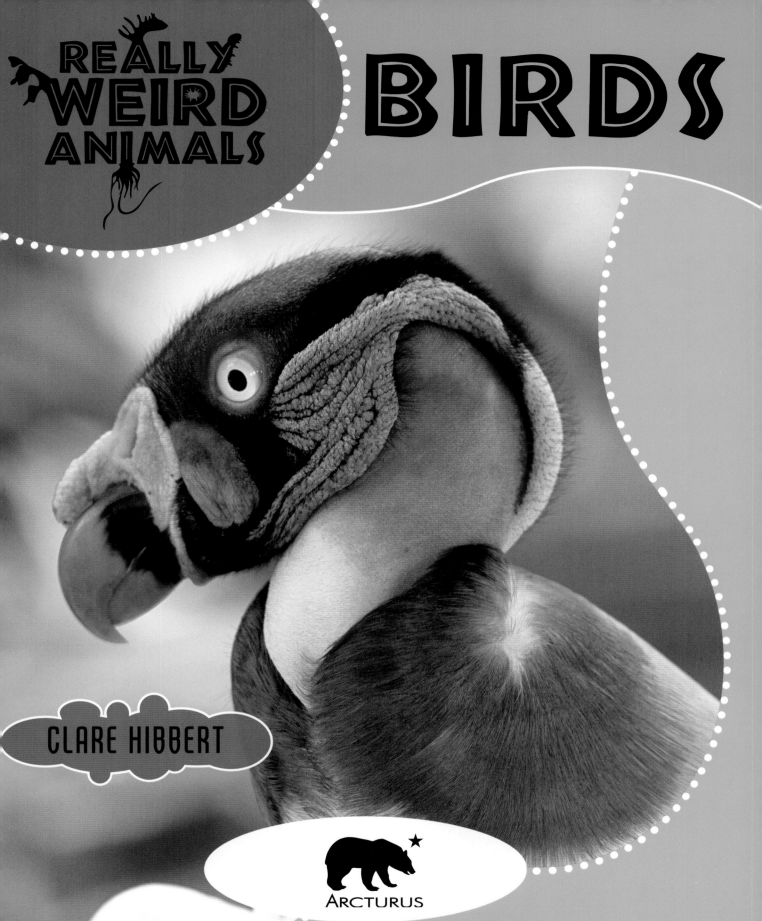

REALLY WEIRD ANIMALS

BIRDS

CLARE HIBBERT

ARCTURUS

This edition first published in 2011 by Arcturus Publishing
Distributed by Black Rabbit Books
P.O. Box 3263
Mankato
Minnesota MN 56002

Printed in China

Series concept: Discovery Books Ltd, 2 College Street, Ludlow, Shropshire SY8 1AN,
www.discoverybooks.net

Managing editor: Paul Humphrey
Editor and picture researcher: Clare Hibbert
Design: sprout.uk.com

Library of Congress Cataloging-in-Publication Data

Hibbert, Clare, 1970-
  Birds / by Clare Hibbert.
      p. cm. -- (Really weird animals)
  Includes index.
  ISBN 978-1-84837-958-9 (library binding)
  1. Birds--Juvenile literature. I. Title.
  QL676.2.H48 2012
  598--dc22
                              2011005600

Photo acknowledgments: Corbis: cover and pp 1 (Wayne Lynch/All Canada Photos), 5 (Wayne
Lynch/All Canada Photos), 14b (Patricia Fogden), 15r (Nigel Pavitt), 18 (James Hager), 25 (Frans
Lanting), 28 (E&P Bauer); FLPA: pp 4 (Sunset), 7tr (Thomas Marent), 14t (Konrad Wothe/Minden
Pictures), 21 (Rob Reijnen/Minden Pictures), 26t (ZSSD/Minden Pictures); iStockphoto: pp 8b
(edurivero), 9l (RichLindie), 9r (SuperKiko), 17 (MindStorm-inc), 19r (Riaanvdb), 20 (RollingEarth),
22bl (johan63), 23br (kkaplin), 24b (Bierchen); Oxford Scientific Films: p 13r (Richard Kirby/
Timeframe Productions Ltd); Photoshot: pp 10 (Andy Rouse), 11b (Ernie Janes), 12 (Andrea Ferrari),
13l (Bruce Beehler), 24t (John Cancalosi), 29t (ANT); Shutterstock: pp 3 (worldswildlifewonders),
6r (szefei), 6b (szefei), 7bl (worldswildlifewonders), 8t (holbox), 11t (TheThirdMan), 15l (hironai),
16l (ClimberJAK), 16br (Leksele), 19l (Villiers Steyn), 22tl (Four Oaks), 22r (Four Oaks), 23t (Wong
Hock weng), 26b (Mihai Dancaescu), 27t (Charidy B), 27b (Braam Collins), 29b (Johan Larson),
31 (TheThirdMan), 32 (Four Oaks).

Cover picture: A king vulture, Panama.

SL001749US
Supplier 04, Date 0411, Print Run 1054

CONTENTS

COCK OF THE ROCK

With their crazy crests, cocks of the rock could be called the punks of the bird world. They're one of the brightest birds in the forests of South America.

WEIRD OR WHAT?

Cocks of the rock are named for their habit of nesting in holes on cliff faces.

COCK OF THE ROCK FACTS

SIZE: around 13 in. long
HOME: tropical and subtropical rain forests, South America
EATS: fruit, insects, small reptiles

Bright colors attract the notice of predators as well as mates. Eagles, hawks, jaguars, and boa constrictors all hunt cocks of the rock.

KING VULTURE

Like many vultures, the king vulture is a scavenger. Having a bald neck and head helps it to avoid getting blood all over its feathers when feasting on carrion.

WEIRD OR WHAT?

King vultures can only croak and wheeze, as they don't have a voice box.

The king vulture is far more colorful than most vultures. The skin on its neck can be orange, red, yellow, or purple.

KING VULTURE FACTS

SIZE: up to 32 in. long
HOME: tropical forests, Central and South America
EATS: carrion

HORNBILL

Hornbills are named for their long, horny beaks. Most of them, including this rhinoceros hornbill, have an odd, helmetlike structure on their bill. Imagine carrying that around on your head all the time!

HORNBILL FACTS

SIZE: 16-64 in. long
HOME: tropical and subtropical Africa and Asia
EATS: fruit, insects, small animals

Hornbills mostly eat fruit. This hornbill is about to gobble down a chunk of juicy papaya.

Hornbill dads imprison their families! The male seals in the female and her eggs to keep them safe from predators. He leaves a small hole to pass food through to his family.

This is a wrinkled hornbill. It's not wrinkly because of old age. The grooves on its beak were there from the moment it hatched.

WEIRD OR WHAT?

Male hornbills sometimes use their beaks to bash rivals—in mid-air!

TOUCAN

Toucans are famous for their impressive beaks, which can make up more than a third of their total body length. That's like you having to walk around with a nose as long as your arm!

TOUCAN FACTS

SIZE: up to 2 ft. long
HOME: tropics of Central and South America
EATS: fruit, insects, frogs, small reptiles, birds

Toucan beaks aren't just long— they're colorful, too. No wonder this species is known as the rainbow-billed toucan.

The choco toucan's beak looks as if it's been dipped in delicious chocolate. Cocoa does grow in the Chocó forests of Colombia where this toucan lives—but the bird feeds on fruit, not cocoa.

WEIRD OR WHAT?

Toucans sometimes prey on songbird eggs and chicks, using their long beaks to delve into nest holes.

The smallest members of the toucan family are toucanets and aracaris. Their beaks may not be as big, but they still look pretty weird. Many aracaris have stripy chest feathers.

Macaroni Penguin

"Here we come!" These macaroni penguins look as if they're skiing. They're stretching out their wings to keep their balance as they race across a glacier.

WEIRD OR WHAT?

Macaroni penguins lay two eggs but they kick the first one out of the nest soon after the second egg is laid.

The macaroni penguin gets its name from its flamboyant, golden crest feathers—in the 18th century, a "macaroni" was a young man who followed the latest fashions slavishly.

MACARONI PENGUIN FACTS

SIZE: 28 in. tall
HOME: around the Southern Ocean
EATS: krill, squid, fish

In summer, macaroni penguins gather together in huge breeding colonies. A colony can contain as many as 100,000 birds. This pair are preening each other.

BIRD of PARADISE

The bird of paradise family includes some of the bird world's biggest show-offs. In many species, like this greater bird of paradise, the males have trailing ornamental feathers, called plumes.

WEIRD OR WHAT?

The loudest bird of paradise is the well-named trumpet bird.

BIRD OF PARADISE FACTS

SIZE: 6-18 in. long
HOME: tropical forests of Australasia, southern Asia, South America
EATS: fruit, spiders

This raggiana bird of paradise male is displaying to attract a mate. He fans out his feathers and prances and bobs. It's lucky the females have a good attention span because these dances can go on for hours.

Wilson's bird of paradise lives in the rain forests of Indonesia. The male's tail plumes form two tight curls. Its body is black with bright splashes of blue, red, and yellow.

Fancy colors are important in the gloomy shade of the rain forest because they catch a female's eye. She knows by looking at his glossy feathers that a male is healthy, and that he'll make a good dad for her chicks.

This has to win the "best nest" award! It's the work of a male bowerbird. He builds a shelter, or bower, out of twigs and grasses.

BOWERBIRD FACTS

SIZE: up to 16 in. long
HOME: forests and scrubland, Australasia
EATS: fruit, flowers, insects

BOWERBIRD

WEIRD OR WHAT?

Some bowerbirds "paint" their bowers. They make the paint from chewed-up leaves and spit.

The bowerbird puts together an eye-catching display to impress his mate. He arranges piles of colorful objects, including shells, fruit, feathers, and even clothespins.

SHOEBILL

The shoebill is a kind of stork. It gets its name from the cloglike shape of its wide, thick bill.

WEIRD OR WHAT?

The shoebill's favorite food are lungfishes—air-breathing fish that live among the plants on the banks of the Nile.

Shoebills are large birds with big appetites. They cruise over rivers and marshes looking for slippery fish, turtles, and even baby crocodiles!

SHOEBILL FACTS

SIZE: 46 in. tall
HOME: wetlands, northeastern Africa
EATS: fish, reptiles

FRIGATE BIRD

Is that red balloon? No—it's the male frigate bird's red throat. This seabird puffs out his throat pouch to attract a mate. The throat can inflate to the size of a human head!

WEIRD OR WHAT?

Frigate birds are amazing fliers. They can stay on the wing for a week at a time.

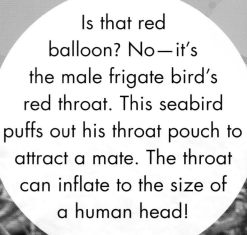

FRIGATE BIRD FACTS

SIZE: 3 ft. long, with a 7.5-ft. wingspan

HOME: tropical and subtropical coastal waters

EATS: fish

Frigate birds usually have one chick. It doesn't look much like its parents when it hatches, though!

BLUE-FOOTED BOOBY

These birds' feet look as if they've stepped in blue paint!

WEIRD OR WHAT?

"Booby" means someone stupid. Early seafarers called these fearless birds boobies because they were very easy to kill.

Blue-footed boobies are masters of fancy footwork. A courting couple performs a funny, jerky dance, moving their feet up and down and sometimes pointing their beaks at the sky.

BLUE-FOOTED BOOBY FACTS

SIZE: 32 in. long
HOME: Pacific Ocean, from California to the Galápagos Islands
EATS: fish, squid

OXPECKER FACTS

SIZE: 8 in. long
HOME: African savannah
EATS: ticks, flies, maggots

"Are you ready for me, sir?" it looks like this oxpecker is saying to the African buffalo. Oxpeckers help to rid many different animals of pests. These helpful little birds land on grazing animals and pick off parasites.

OXPECKER

Pampering has its risks. Oxpeckers have such sharp, pointy beaks they sometimes open old cuts or make new ones. "Hold still, now!"

Oxpeckers perform another handy job for their hosts. They hiss when they are alarmed, which makes them useful lookouts. This giraffe will soon know if a predator is approaching.

WEIRD OR WHAT?

Oxpeckers sometimes feed on their host's dandruff and even their earwax. How disgusting!

FLAMINGO

FLAMINGO FACTS

SIZE: up to 5 ft. tall
HOME: lakes and coastal areas in
      warm parts of the world
EATS: blue-green algae

Why do flamingos look so funny when they walk? Their legs seem to bend the wrong way!

The parts that look like a flamingo's feet are their toes, what look like the lower legs are feet, and what look like knees are actually ankles.

WEIRD OR WHAT?

It's not snacking on shrimp that makes flamingos pink. A pigment in the blue-green algae they eat colors their flamboyant feathers.

All birds' legs are jointed like this, but flamingos' long legs make them look especially comical!

RED-CROWNED CRANE

These crazy cranes appear to be singing a duet! They're performing their mating dance, which consists of a series of bows, head bobbing, and leaps.

RED-CROWNED CRANE FACTS

SIZE: 56 in. tall
HOME: East Asian wetlands
EATS: frogs, insects, plants

WEIRD OR WHAT?

Red-crowned cranes are the heaviest cranes. Males can weigh as much as 30 pounds—that's about the same as ten chickens.

Cranes mate for life. They don't just dance at the start of the breeding season. They like to do it at other times of the year, too.

Weaver Bird

Weaver birds are the champion architects of the bird world. They collect grasses or reeds in their beaks, then use them to weave amazingly intricate nests.

This bright yellow fellow is a cape weaver. See how his nest takes shape. The entrance is at the bottom, to keep it hidden from airborne predators.

①

②

③

WEAVER BIRD FACTS

SIZE: about 8 in. long
HOME: sub-Saharan Africa, parts of Asia and Australia
EATS: seeds, grain, insects

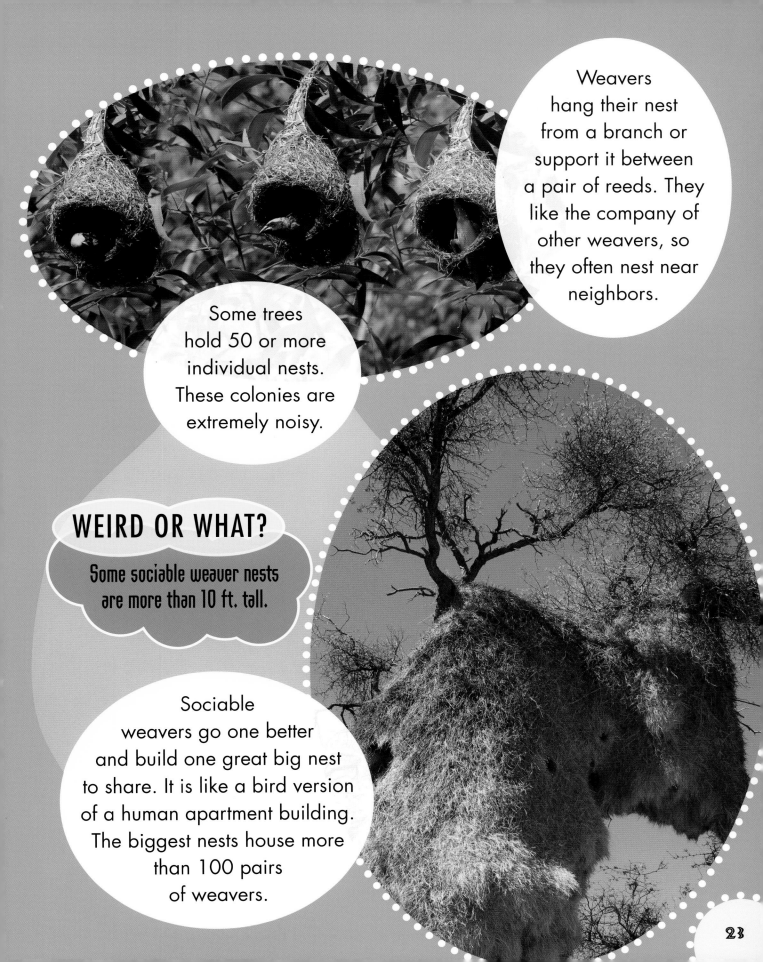

Weavers hang their nest from a branch or support it between a pair of reeds. They like the company of other weavers, so they often nest near neighbors.

Some trees hold 50 or more individual nests. These colonies are extremely noisy.

WEIRD OR WHAT?

Some sociable weaver nests are more than 10 ft. tall.

Sociable weavers go one better and build one great big nest to share. It is like a bird version of a human apartment building. The biggest nests house more than 100 pairs of weavers.

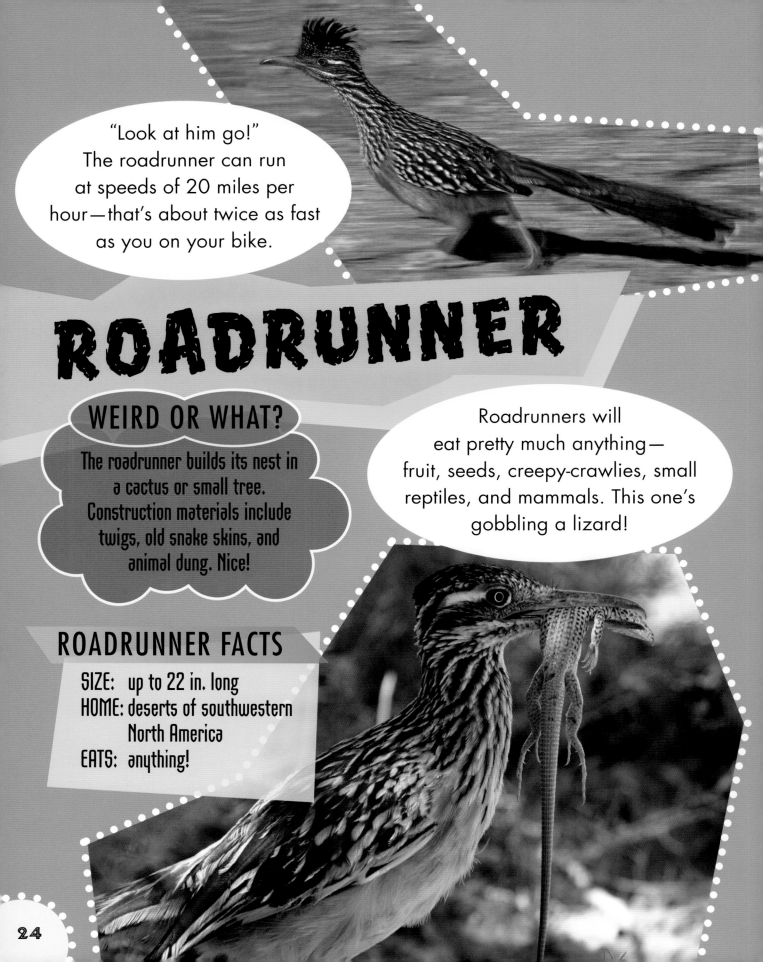

"Look at him go!" The roadrunner can run at speeds of 20 miles per hour—that's about twice as fast as you on your bike.

ROADRUNNER

WEIRD OR WHAT?

The roadrunner builds its nest in a cactus or small tree. Construction materials include twigs, old snake skins, and animal dung. Nice!

Roadrunners will eat pretty much anything—fruit, seeds, creepy-crawlies, small reptiles, and mammals. This one's gobbling a lizard!

ROADRUNNER FACTS

SIZE: up to 22 in. long
HOME: deserts of southwestern North America
EATS: anything!

Kakapo

A parrot that can't fly—surely not? The kakapo is an extremely rare parrot that lives in New Zealand. It hunts at night, relying on its sense of smell to find prey. Whiskers on either side of its beak help it to feel its way.

WEIRD OR WHAT?

The kakapo lost its ability to fly millions of years ago—probably because there weren't any large land predators in its island home.

KAKAPO FACTS

SIZE: 26 in. long
HOME: New Zealand
EATS: leaves, seeds, fruit

PELICAN

Pelicans' beaks are like nature's fishing nets. These birds have super-stretchy throat pouches, which they use to scoop fish out of the water.

PELICAN FACTS

SIZE: 40-76 in. long, depending on species
HOME: warm, watery regions worldwide
EATS: fish

WEIRD OR WHAT?

A pelican's pouch can hold more than 20 pounds of fish—three times more fish than the bird has space for in its stomach!

There are about eight species of pelican. These white pelicans live in North America. Like all pelicans, they fly well and are also strong swimmers.

The secretary bird is named for its distinctive black crest feathers. These feathers look like the quill pens that secretaries used long ago and tucked behind their ears.

Secretary Bird

Thanks to its long legs the secretary bird is a speedy hunter. It kills its favorite food—snakes—by stamping them to death!

WEIRD OR WHAT?

The secretary bird's scaly legs protect it against snake bites.

SECRETARY BIRD FACTS

SIZE: 52 in. tall, with a wingspan of more than 6 ft.
HOME: African savannah
EATS: snakes, lizards, grasshoppers, mice, birds' eggs

POTOO

"Aaaghhh!"
This is the strangled cry coming out of the potoo's gaping mouth. Potoos make funny barking noises, too.

WEIRD OR WHAT?

The potoo has slits in its eyelids—so it can see with its eyes shut!

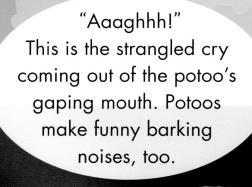

The potoo's brown, mottled feathers disguise it to look like part of a tree. This camouflage hides it by day when it's resting. At night it hunts beetles, moths, and other insects.

POTOO FACTS

SIZE: 14 in. long
HOME: tropical and subtropical forests of South America
EATS: insects

TAWNY FROGMOUTH

How many birds can you see? With such excellent camouflage, it's hard to spot the two chicks that this proud parent is guarding!

WEIRD OR WHAT?

The frogmouth gets its name from its wide mouth, not because it eats frogs (although it might make a snack of one very occasionally!).

FROGMOUTH FACTS

SIZE: up to 20 in. long
HOME: southern Asia and Australasia
EATS: insects, small lizards, mice, berries

Like its cousin, the potoo, a tawny frogmouth relies on its coloring to blend in with a branch. If it feels threatened it freezes—being motionless completes the disguise.

GLOSSARY

alga (plural algae) One of a group of living things that include seaweeds and some plankton.

carrion The meat (flesh) of a dead animal.

colony A group of animals or other living things of the same species that set up home in the same place.

courting The behavior that leads up to mating. Many birds have elaborate courtship rituals involving song, dance, and displays of plumage.

glacier A large, very slow-moving mass of ice.

inflate Blow up with air.

krill Very small, shrimplike crustaceans.

mammal An animal with a backbone that is warm-blooded, has fur, and feeds its young on mother's milk.

parasite A living thing that does not produce or find its own food, but instead lives on a host that it relies on for food.

pigment Coloring.

predator An animal that hunts and kills other animals for food.

prey An animal that is hunted and killed by another animal for food.

rain forest A forest habitat where rain falls almost every day. In a tropical rain forest, the climate is hot and steamy all year round.

reptile A cold-blooded animal with a backbone. Reptiles are covered in scales and usually lay eggs on land (although some reptiles in cooler climates give birth to live young).

savannah Tropical grassland.

scavenger A meat-eating animal that doesn't kill its own prey, but instead feeds on the leftover flesh of animals killed by other predators, or on animals that have died of natural causes.

scrubland An area where grass and shrubs grow, but few trees.

species One particular type of living thing. Members of the same species look similar and can reproduce together in the wild.

subtropical Describes the regions of the earth that lie between tropical and temperate areas.

tropical Describes the warm part of the world near the equator (the imaginary line that circles the middle of the earth).

wetlands Habitats where the land is wet and boggy.

wingspan The distance from wing tip to wing tip when a bird stretches out its wings.

FURTHER INFORMATION

Books

A Hummingbird's Story: How I Came to Be by Barbara Kurtz (CreateSpace, 2011)

Birds by Maurice Pledger (Silver Dolphin, 2010)

Birds of a Feather by Jane Yolen (Wordsong, 2011)

National Geographic Field Guide to Birds of North America (National Geographic, 2006

Those Pesky Penguins by Sarah Cussen (Pineapple Press, 2011)

DVDs

David Attenborough's Life of Birds (BBC/PBS, 1998)
March of the Penguins (Warner Home Video, 2006)

Web Sites

BBC Wildlife Finder
http://www.bbc.co.uk/nature/class/Bird

National Audubon Society
http://www.audubon.org

National Geographic: Birds
http://animals.nationalgeographic.com/
animals/birding/bird-photos/

Natural History Museum
http://www.nhm.ac.uk/nature-online/life/
birds/index.html

The Life of Birds
http://www.pbs.org/lifeofbirds/

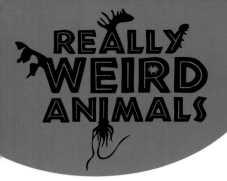

INDEX